IN THE BEGINNING

BEGINNING

ADAM to ABRAHAM

IN THE BEGINNING: ADAM TO ABRAHAM

ISBN: 978-1-941173-35-0
American Edition

Published by

Olive Press Messianic and Christian Publisher

olivepresspublisher.com

Printed in the USA

This book is dedicated to children of
all languages and nations.

*"For You formed my inward parts; You covered me in my
mother's womb. I will praise You, for I am fearfully and
wonderfully made;" Psalm 139:13-14*

INTRODUCTION

Adam and Eve lived in the beautiful Garden of Eden. They had a very special friendship with God and everything was just perfect.

They could eat any of the fruit growing in the garden, except from one tree in the center of the garden. Its fruit would bring death.

Yet Adam and Eve chose to disobey God and ate the forbidden fruit. Instantly everything changed. The **darkness** of sin and death had entered God's perfect creation.

So God sent Adam and Eve away from His *light* and peaceful garden. But He promised that He would send His Son. He would save people from sin and death. Then they would live forever with their Creator.

The First Day

When God made the earth,
it was **dark**.

Then God said,
"Let there be *light*";
(Genesis 1:3)
So it was done and there was *light*!

God saw that the light was good,
so He separated the *light*
from the **darkness**.
God called the *light* Day,
and the **darkness** He called Night.

*In the beginning was the Word, and the Word
was with God, and the Word was God.*
(John 1:1)

The Second Day

Then God said,
"Let there be a firmament in the
midst of the waters, and let it divide
the waters from the waters."
(Genesis 1:6)
God made the firmament and called it Heaven.
So there was water under the sky
and water above the sky.

He was in the beginning with God. (John 1:2)

The Third Day

Then God said,

"Let the waters under the heavens be
gathered together into one place, and let
the dry land appear";
(Genesis 1:9)

And so, it was done. And God named
the dry land Earth and the waters Seas.

Then God said,

"Let the earth bring forth grass, the herb
that yields seed, and the fruit tree that
yields fruit according to its kind, whose
seed is in itself, on the earth";
(Genesis 1:11)

So, it happened and the earth was green!
And God saw that all this was good.

*All things were made through Him, and
without Him nothing was made that was made.* (John 1:3)

The Fourth Day

Then God said,

"Let there be lights in the firmament of the heavens to divide the day from night; and let them be for signs and seasons, and for days and years; and let them be for lights in the firmament of the heavens to give *light* on the earth";

(Genesis 1:14-15)

The sun was the brightest *light* and ruled over the day,
and the pale moon ruled over the night.
God also made the stars, too many to count.

In this way, God separated the *light* from the
darkness and He saw that it was good.

In Him was life, and the life was the light of men.
(John 1:4)

The Fifth Day

Then God said,

"Let the waters abound with an abundance
of living creatures, and let birds fly above
the earth across the face of the firmament
of the heavens."
(Genesis 1:20)

So, God created every kind of living creature in
the sea and every species of bird. God saw that
this was good and He blessed them, saying,

"Be fruitful and multiply, and fill the waters
in the seas, and let birds
multiply on the earth."
(Genesis 1:22)

The Sixth Day

Then God said,

"Let the earth bring forth the living creature
according to its kind: cattle and creeping
thing and beast of the earth, each
according to its kind";   (Genesis 1:24)

God made all the different kinds of animals and each kind of animal
had offspring, just like themselves.
And God saw that this was good.

Then God said,

"Let Us make man in Our image, according to Our likeness;
let them have dominion over the fish of the sea,
over the birds of the air, and over the cattle,
over all the earth
and over every creeping thing that
creeps on the earth."   (Genesis 1:26)

So God formed man from the dust of the ground, and when God breathed life into his nostrils, he became a living person.

Then the LORD God planted a garden in Eden and He put the man there to look after it.

The garden had many beautiful trees and each type of tree had its own kind of delicious fruit. In the middle of the garden there was the tree of life, and the tree of the knowledge of good and evil. A river flowed through the garden and watered it.

The LORD God told the man that he could eat from any of the trees in the garden. Except from the tree of the knowledge of good and evil. If he ate the fruit from that tree he would die!

God said it was not good for man to be alone. He would make Adam a helper, someone just like himself. God brought every kind of animal and bird He had made to the man, and he chose names for them.

Each living creature had a mate just like themselves. Yet there was no-one like Adam.

So God put the man into a deep sleep and removed one of his ribs. Then God used the rib to make a woman. When God brought her to the man, he was delighted. At last he had a mate, someone just like himself!

Each kind of lovely flower growing in the garden had its own special perfume and every kind of bird had its unique song. Each kind of animal had a different language. So, the garden was filled with delightful smells, beautiful birdsongs, and the chatter of busy animals.

Adam and Eve could speak, see, hear, smell, taste and touch; and they enjoyed everything that God had made. They also had a free will, to make their own choices and decisions. Adam and Eve were innocent and even though they were naked, they were not ashamed.

God blessed Adam and Eve. He told them to have many children and rule over all that He had made. The fish in the sea, the birds in the sky, and every living creature that moves on the earth.

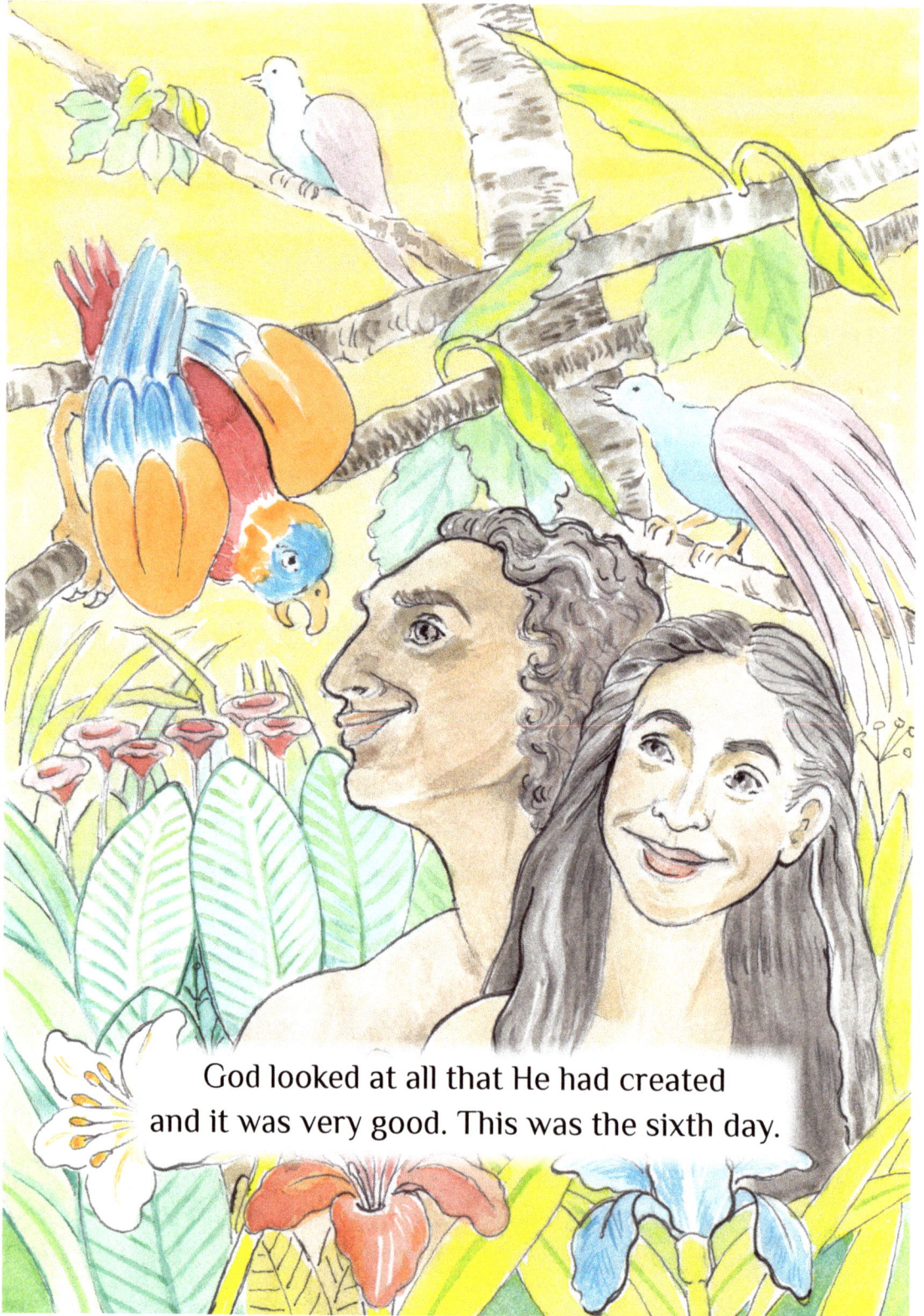

God looked at all that He had created
and it was very good. This was the sixth day.

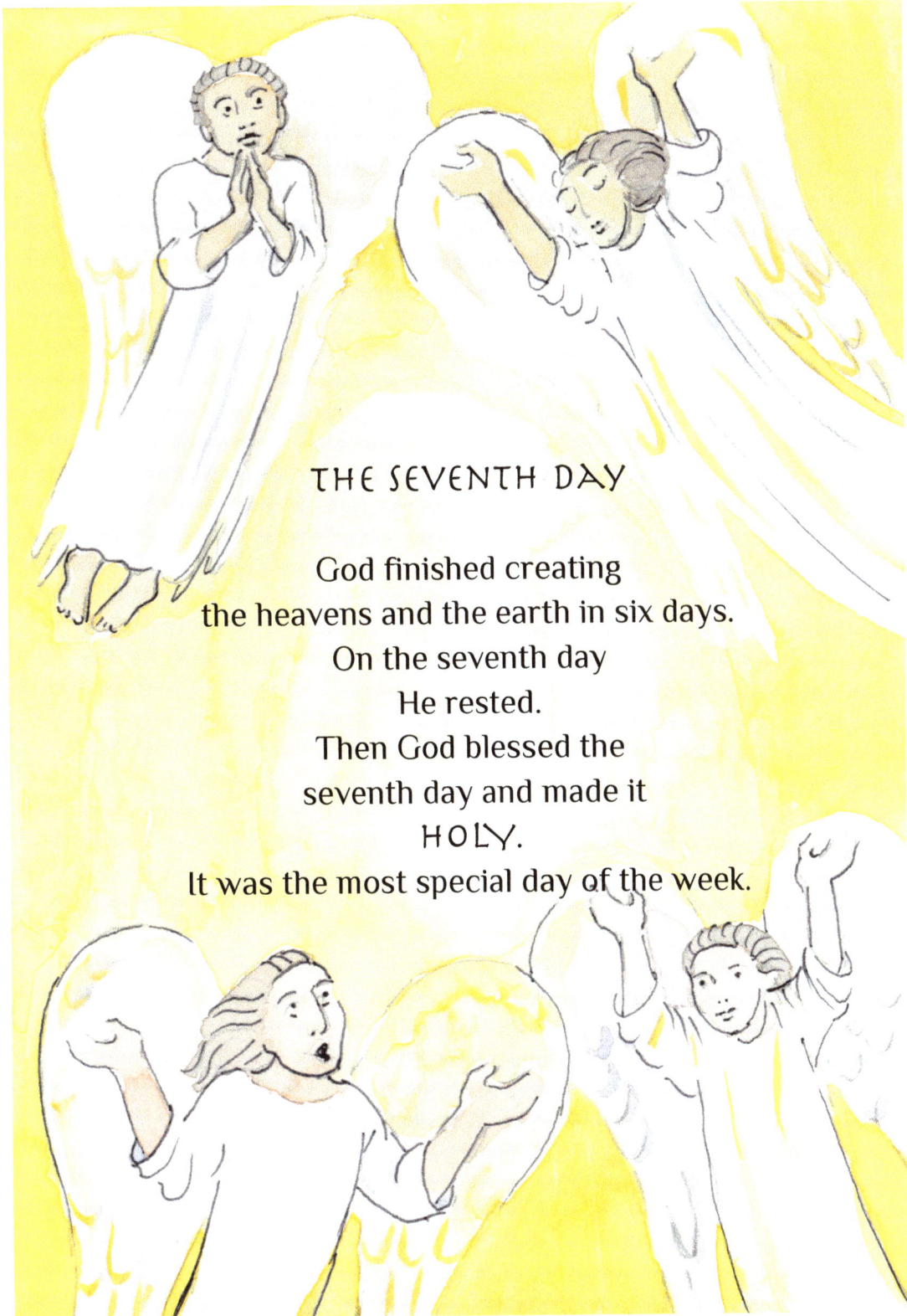

THE SEVENTH DAY

God finished creating
the heavens and the earth in six days.
On the seventh day
He rested.
Then God blessed the
seventh day and made it
HOLY.
It was the most special day of the week.

The Crafty Serpent

Now the serpent was more cunning than any of the beast of the field which the LORD God had made. And he asked the woman, "Has God indeed said, 'You shall not eat of every tree of the garden'?"(Genesis 3:1)

The woman said that they could eat from all the trees, except from the tree in the middle of the garden. God had told them not to eat its fruit, nor touch it, or they would die.

Then the serpent said to the woman, "You will not surely die. For God knows that in the day you eat of it your eyes will be opened, and you will be like God, knowing good and evil." (Genesis 3:4-5)

"When he (Satan) speaks a lie, he speaks from his own resources,
for he is a liar and the father (originator) of it."
(John 8:44b)

Eve believed the serpent's lie. She looked at the tree and saw that it was beautiful. Its fruit was good for food and would also make her wise. So, she took some of the fruit and ate it! Then she gave some to her husband and he ate it.

Instantly, Adam and Eve lost their innocence. Their eyes were opened and for the first time they knew that they were naked. Then they were ashamed and sewed fig leaves together to cover themselves.

When they heard God walking in the garden in the cool of the day, they hid among the trees in the **darkness**.

Then the LORD God called to Adam and said to him, "Where are you?" (Genesis 3:9)

Adam said he had heard God walking in the garden and was afraid because he was naked, and hid himself.

God asked who had told him he was naked. Had he eaten from the tree he had been commanded not to eat from?

Then Adam blamed the woman that God had given him. He said that she had given him the fruit, and so he ate it.

When God asked the woman what she had done, she blamed the serpent. She said that he had deceived her, so she ate the fruit.

Then God cursed the serpent. He would no longer proudly lift himself up, but crawl on his belly and eat dust all the days of his life.

God said that the serpent and his offspring would be enemies of the woman and her offspring. But He promised that a descendant of the woman would defeat the serpent.

There had been no death, no pain, no fear and no sadness in God's perfect creation. But because of Adam and Eve's sin, these things came into the world. So now Eve would know suffering and sadness in having children.

God told Adam that the ground was cursed because of his sin, and would produce thorns and thistles. Adam would work hard to provide food from the fields, until he died. Then he would return to the soil from which he was taken.

God knew that Adam and Eve had both chosen to disobey Him. Yet He made tunics for them from animal skins. It was the first time that blood had been shed in God's perfect creation and He was heartbroken.

If Adam and Eve ate the fruit from the tree of life, they would live forever in sin. So God drove them out of the garden of Eden. Then He placed angels and a flaming sword which turned in every direction, to guard the way to the tree of life.

Now Adam and Eve had to work hard to survive. Instead of God caring for all their needs, they had to look after themselves. One sin led to other sins. Like a dark cloud, they blocked the *light* of God's pure love from shining on them.

In the cool of the evening, Adam and Eve remembered their talks with God in the garden of Eden. Then sometimes the breeze seemed to carry a sad song, reminding them of what they had lost.

I made you, I formed you,
From the dust of the earth.
I gave you life,
You are Mine.
Father and beloved child.

You turned away, broke My law,
Adam where are you?
Do not hide,
You are Mine.
Father and beloved child.

Turn to Me, come back to Me,
All I have is yours.
I will dry your tears,
You are Mine.
Father and beloved child.

Cain and Abel

Adam and Eve had two sons. The firstborn was named Cain and the younger son was called Abel. Cain became a farmer and Abel kept sheep.

One day the two brothers brought an offering to God. Cain gave some crops from the ground, and Abel gave the firstborn of his flock. God respected Abel and accepted his offering. But Cain and his offering did not please God.

Then Cain was angry and bitter. But God said there was no reason to sulk. Cain could choose to do what was right and be accepted. Or he could choose not to do right, then he would be tempted to sin.

Now Cain didn't listen to God's advice. He invited Abel to go out to the field and while they were there, he killed him. When God asked where his brother was, Cain said he didn't know; and anyway, was it his job to take care of his brother?

Then God cursed Cain. He had spilled his innocent brother's blood on the earth and so it would no longer provide food for him. He would be a fugitive and a homeless wanderer on the earth.

Cain was not at all sorry for his crime, but he was very upset by his punishment. He was driven from the land and God's presence; and as he wandered the earth, he feared that someone might kill him.

So God put a mark on Cain, that would warn anyone he met not to kill him. Then Cain left God's presence and eventually he settled in the land of Nod, east of Eden.

"You are of your father the devil, and the desires of your father you want to do. He was a murderer from the beginning, and does not stand in the truth, because there is no truth in him." (John 8:44a)

Adam and Eve
|
Cain   Abel   Seth

Seth

Eve grieved over her wicked son Cain and mourned for her good son Abel.

Then God gave her another son to take Abel's place, and Adam named him Seth.

After Seth was born, Adam had more sons and daughters.

Seth was a good man and he had a son named Enosh. Then people began to pray to the LORD.

But Cain and his descendants were wicked and chose to hide away from the *light* of God's presence.

> *And the light shines in the darkness,*
> *and the darkness did not comprehend it.*
> *(John 1:5)*

Adam and Eve
|
Cain   Abel   Seth
|
Enosh
|
Cainan
|
Mahalalel
|
Jared
|
Enoch
|
Methuselah
|
Lamech
|

Noah

Noah

As time went on, mankind moved further and further away from God's *light,* until the world became a **dark** and violent place. Then God was sorry that He had created human beings.

Yet even in those wicked times, there was one man who pleased God. His name was Noah and he had three sons, Shem, Ham, and Japheth.

God warned Noah that He was going to flood the earth and told him to build an ark four hundred and fifty feet long, seventy-five feet wide, and forty-five feet high, with rooms inside and three decks. It had to be large enough to carry Noah, his family, and two of every kind of animal and bird, and all the food they would need.

Noah began building immediately, following the plans God had given him. It took a long time and many people came to see his colossal boat. Then Noah would warn them that God was going to flood the earth. But they just laughed at him!

The Flood

Finally, the ark was finished, and Noah and his family went inside. Then the animals and birds followed him, two by two. God waited patiently until they were all safely on board, then shut the door behind them.

Immediately the sky darkened and rain poured down. The underground fountains also burst open and soon the boat was lifted off the earth. The waters grew higher and higher, until the tallest mountain was covered!

Every living creature on earth was drowned.

Only Noah and those with him survived. It was crowded, noisy, and smelly on board, but all the passengers were safe.

A New Beginning

Then God remembered Noah and sent a wind to blow over the earth. He shut off the underground fountains and stopped the rain.

As the flood waters slowly receded, the ark came to rest on the mountains of Ararat. Noah waited forty days and then he opened the window of the ark. He sent out a raven and it flew about, waiting for the floodwaters to dry up.

Noah also sent out a dove, but there was no place where she could perch. So she flew back to the ark, and Noah took her inside. After seven more days, he sent the dove out again. This time she returned to him with a freshly plucked olive leaf in her beak.

Noah waited another seven days and sent the dove out again. This time she did not come back. Then Noah knew that the floodwaters had gone. But he waited two more months for the ground to dry. Then God told Noah to leave the ark, with his family and all the living creatures.

Noah was very grateful to God for saving them all. So he built an altar to thank God with burnt offerings.

God's Promise

God was pleased with Noah's devotion and promised that He would never destroy life on earth again with a flood. Then He put a brightly colored rainbow in the sky, as a reminder of His promise.

God blessed Noah and his three sons, commanding them to multiply and re-populate the earth.

Shem, Ham, and Japheth had offspring and God was kind to them all. Yet His special favor was on Shem and his descendants. God had great plans in mind for them.

The Tower of Babel

Descendants of Noah traveled from the east and came to a spacious plain in the land of Shinar. It was watered by two rivers and was very fertile.

Now God had commanded the people to separate and re-populate the earth. Yet, just like Adam and Eve, they chose to disobey God and settled together in the plain.

They made bricks and built a city with a high tower, reaching into the heavens. They hoped they would become famous and prevent God from scattering them across the earth.

When God saw them building, He knew they had joined together to rebel against Him. United together and speaking one language, there were no limits to what they might do!

So God decided to confuse their speech. Suddenly, they began speaking in different languages, and could not understand one another at all!

Well, after that, it was impossible for them to work together. So they began to move apart in all directions. In this way, God scattered the people all over the world.

Noah
|
Shem
|
Arphaxad
|
Shelah
|
Eber
|
Reu
|
Serug
|
Nahor
|
Terah
|
Abraham

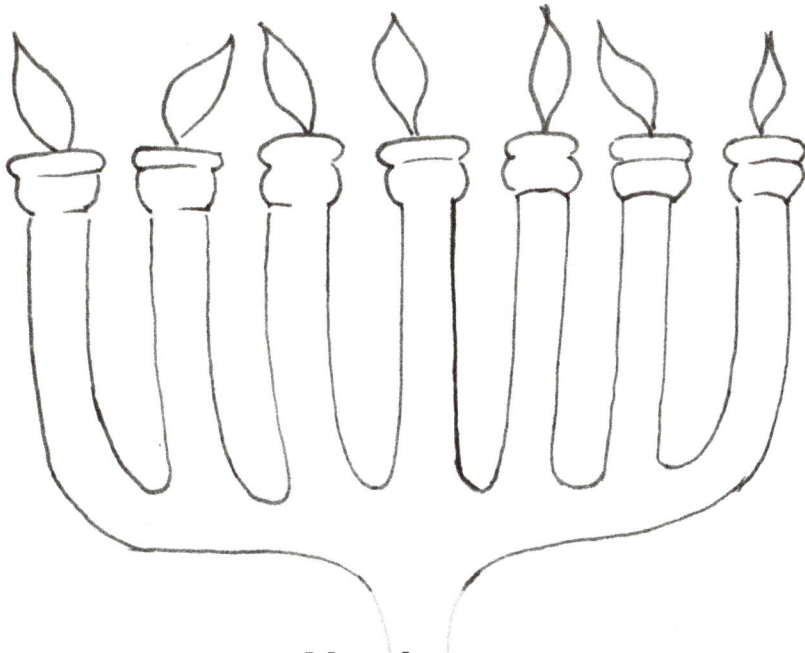

Abraham

With the passing of time, every nation chose to worship other gods and to live in **darkness**. So God decided that He would create a new nation.

This nation would be like His firstborn son. They would be faithful to Him and be like a shining *light* in the **dark** world.

God chose Abraham, a descendant of Shem, to become the father of this new nation.

You can read about Abraham's adventures with God in another story!

REVIEWS

Good books help us to think. Children need to know the importance of thinking God's way rather than the world's way. They need to know how their decisions, both good and bad, will affect their lives just like Adam & Eve's, Cain's, and other Bible characters. This book shows God's holiness and mercy, right from the beginning. Pauline quotes Scripture, which is so important as many parents today think the Bible is obsolete and outdated. The beautiful illustrations will remain in the children's minds for years to come.

> Lois Rykse, married to Mel, and great grandmother to 33 children
> Michigan, USA

As a friend and former colleague of Pauline, I am honoured to be writing a review of In The Beginning. Pauline has captured the Biblical content along with such beautiful illustrations, bringing it alive for the child reader or like me the Dad reading it with his children.

Pauline is a gifted author putting pictures into words and words into pictures. My daughter just loves her books and it thrills me to see children excited about the Word of God. In this book children are shown (and we adults reminded) how it all began, and what an awesome God we have.

> Colin A McFarland, married to Kicki, father of two children
> Northern Ireland (formerly lived in Israel)

As a grandparent and retired primary school teacher, in both the Uk and Spain. I find this book of Pauline Shone's an excellent way of introducing young people to the often complex stories of the Old Testament, particularly in our multi faith world. They are easy to read or "show and tell" due to the charming and detailed illustrations, which open up opportunities to extend children's vocabularies and verbal expression. I heartily recommend it.

> Sally, married to Ian Isaacs
> Manchester, England (formerly lived in Menorca, Spain)

I hope you enjoyed this book.
And remember, God made you and loves you.

Pauline Shone